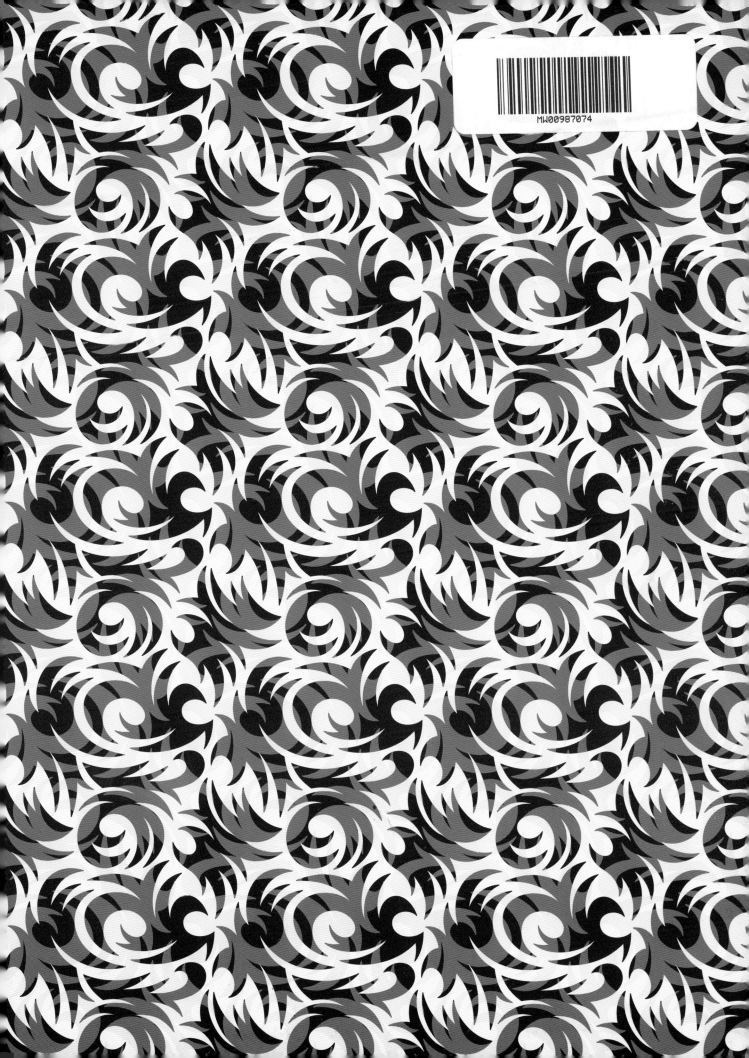

DEDICATION

Dedicated to all MUcaws, past, present and future.

ACKNOWLEDGMENTS

Kristin Blackwood

Sage Blackwood

Sheila Tarr

Mike Blanc

MUcaw
VanitaBooks, LLC

Illustration and design by Mike Blanc.
ISBN 978-1-938164-22-4
Printed in China.

www.VanitaBooks.com

MUCAW

STORY BY VANITA OELSCHLAGER

WITH ART BY MIKE BLANC

UNIVERSITY *of*
MOUNT
UNION
Be Exceptional

University of Mount Union
1972 Clark Avenue
Alliance, Ohio 44601
800 334 6682

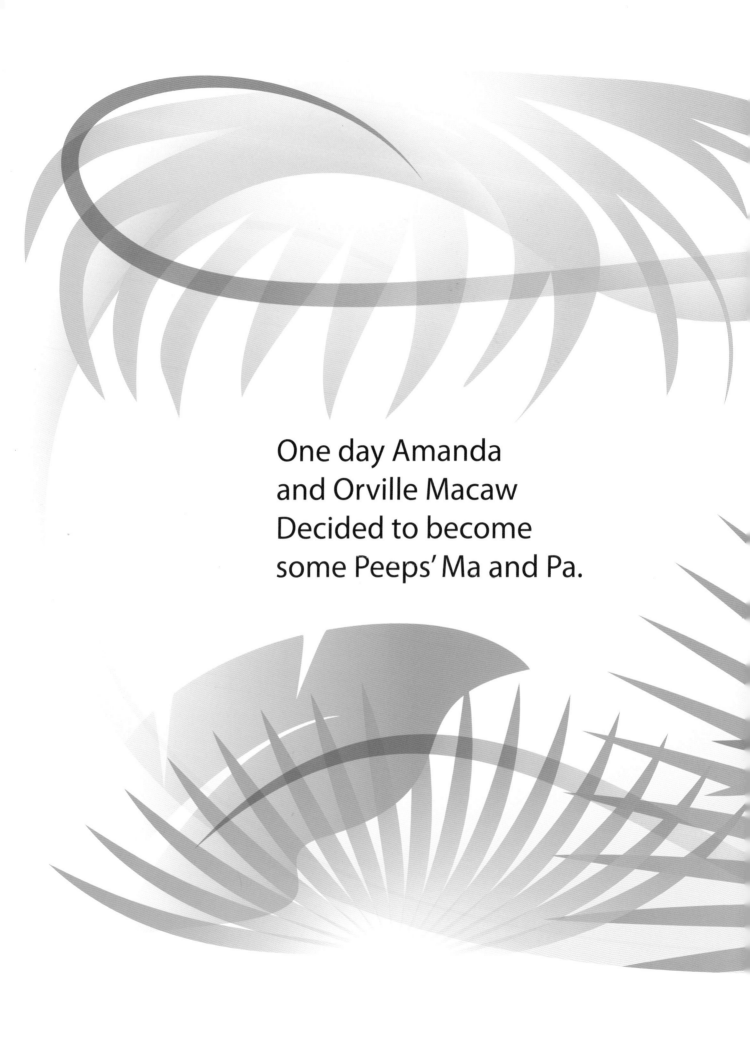

One day Amanda
and Orville Macaw
Decided to become
some Peeps' Ma and Pa.

They soon worked hard
at filling their nest.
But one of their eggs
was not like the rest.

It was so big it crowded
out all of the others.
They knew he'd be bigger
than his sisters and brothers.

They waited and waited
for the eggs to crack.
And they did, one by one,
but the big egg stayed back.

The other babies waited
for a sister or brother.
As they started to play
and have fun with each other.

And then in while
they heard a loud 'crack'.
Something came out
and the babies skittered back.

Their brother appeared
after a lot of work.
This peep struggled out
with a twist, bump and jerk.

Ma and Pa and the kids
were full of surprise.
Their brother had long legs
and was a much bigger size.

It was hard not to stare
at the giant macaw.
Other birds in the hood
couldn't believe what they saw.

While Ma and Pa treated him
just like the others.
They had to feed him
much more than his brothers.

All of their peeps would grow
to learn their own song.
But how could this baby
fit in or belong?

Well this macaw grew up
much better than they thought.
He got a great job
as Mount Union's mascot!

So here's to you kids
when you go to a game.
Look for MUcaw
and yell out his name.

Give him a 'hug'
and a 'yay' and a 'whoot'.
Tell him you love him
and you think he's real cute.

Tell him when you grow up
you'll be back at Mount,
To get your education there,
on that he can count.

AND NOW, TO LEARN MORE ABOUT
MUCAW...TURN THE PAGE. ➤

WHO IS MUCAW?

In 2018, MUcaw celebrates his 25th birthday representing the University of Mount Union.

25

Happy Birthday!

In these 25 years, he has been much more than a face for the school.

A DAY IN THE LIFE.

MUcaw is a very busy bird. He likes to go to football games and cheer on the team. He pops up at some admission events and other sports games. He loves to cheer people on and bring up their spirits.

When MUcaw isn't cheering for his friends, he is doing nice things for others!

On MUcaw's 10th anniversary he donated lots of toys to children in need.

THE CHOICE.

WHY MUCAW CHOSE THE UNIVERSITY OF MOUNT UNION

The University of Mount Union consistently ranks among the top colleges and universities in the Midwest.

Orville Hartshorn started Mount Union in 1846 with the hope of accepting many different types of students.

KEEP IT GREEN.

MORE REASONS WHY
MUCAW LOVES THE UMU

MUcaw loves the environment, so Mount Union's ongoing effort to raise awareness for recycling makes MUcaw very happy.

Not only do they raise awareness, they take part in recycling all over campus.

All of this is to create a sustainable, efficient, and healthy atmosphere where everyone can learn, grow and work!

ABOUT THE AUTHOR
VANITA (BAUKNIGHT '63) OELSCHLAGER

VANITA is a wife, mother, grandmother, philanthropist, former teacher, current caregiver, author and poet. She is a graduate of the University of Mount Union in Alliance, Ohio, where she currently serves as a Trustee. Vanita is also Writer in Residence for the Literacy Program at The University of Akron. She and her husband Jim received a Lifetime Achievement Award from the National Multiple Sclerosis Society in 2006. She won the Congressional Angels in Adoption™ Award for the State of Ohio in 2007 and was named National Volunteer of the Year by the MS Society in 2008. She was honored as 2009 Woman Philanthropist of the Year by the United Way of Summit County. In May 2011, Vanita received an honorary Doctor of Humane Letters from the University of Mount Union.

ABOUT THE ARTIST MIKE BLANC

Mike is an author and award-winning illustrator of children's literature. Books with Vanita include The Gandy Dancers, The Pullman Porters, Postcards from a War and Bonyo Bonyo, The True Story of a Brave Boy from Kenya, created with associate artist, Kristin Blackwood. In 2016, Mike wrote and illustrated Cimarron Girl, The Dust Bowl Years of Abigail Brubaker.